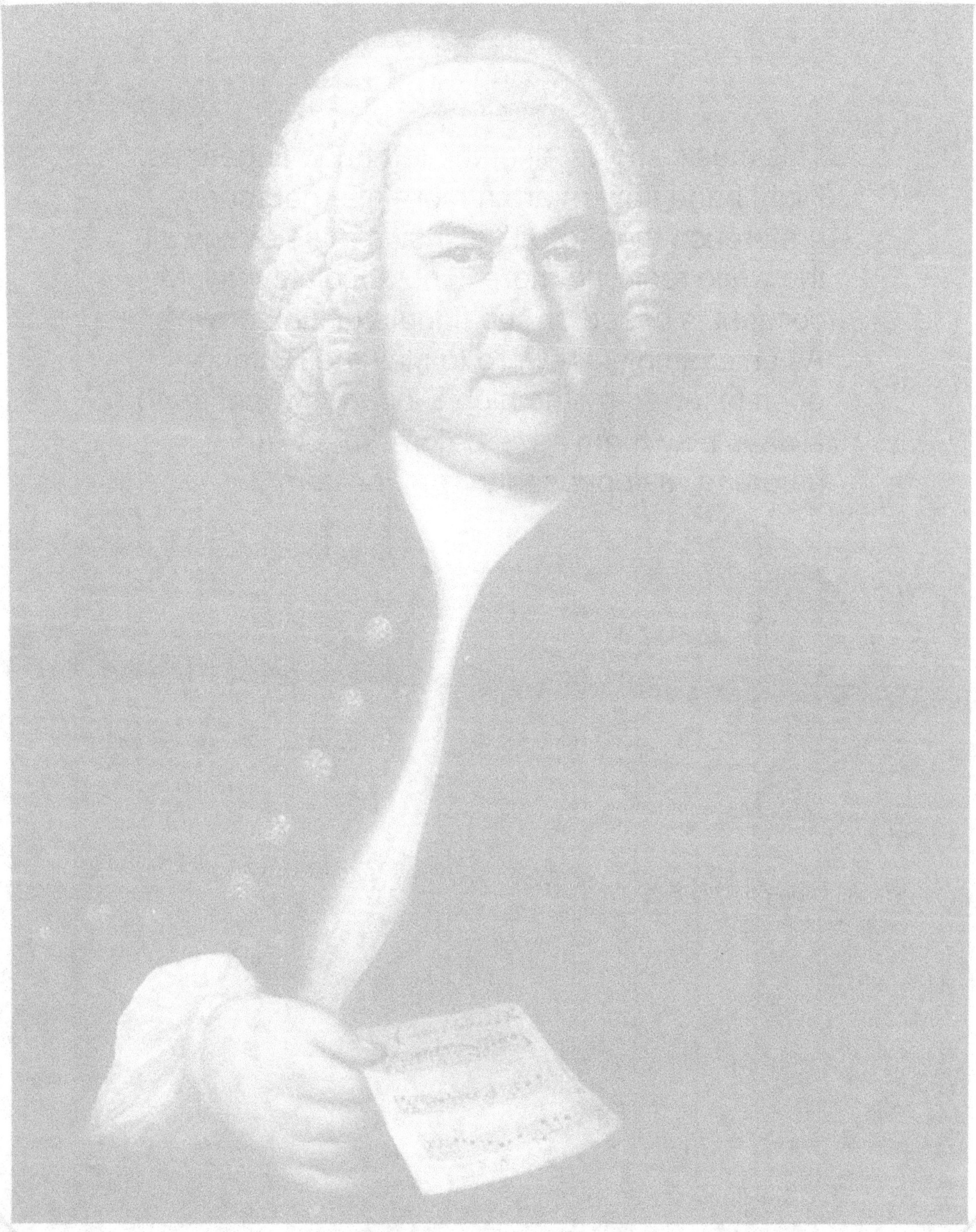

This music shows all of the left hand fingerings. Right hand fingers are a more of a personal preference therefore I've shown my strategy all the while realizing there is no absolute way. My concept is based on "no fingers upside down". As an example, if I were to play the B string open followed by the high E open, I would try to always play them as "i" before "m" or "m" before "a" as opposed to "m-i" or "a-m".

BWV 911 in Em

Fugue
J.S.Bach

Standard tuning

♩ = 60

N-Gt

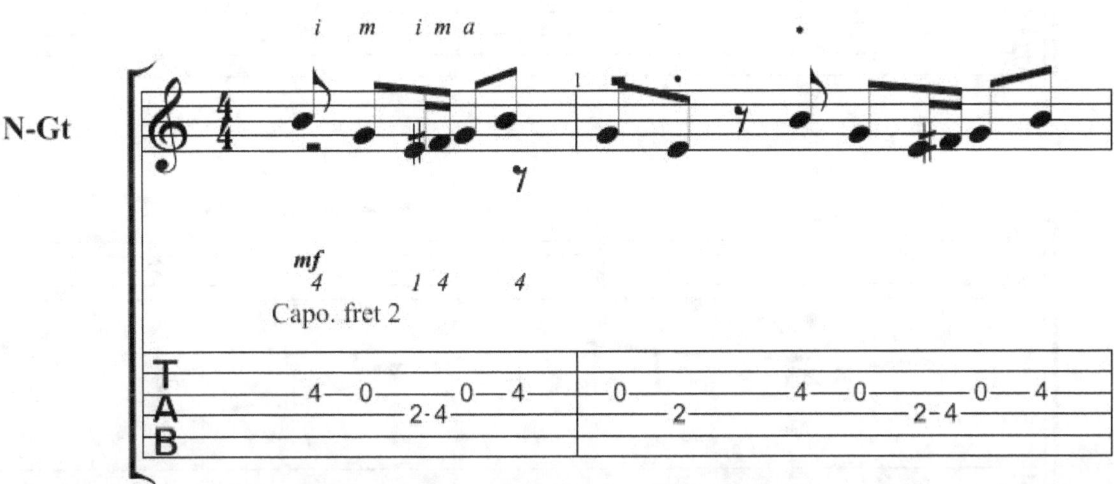

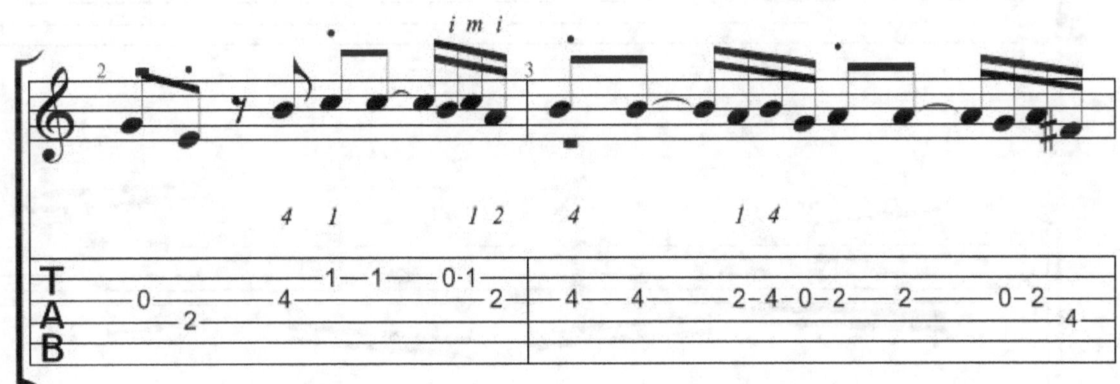

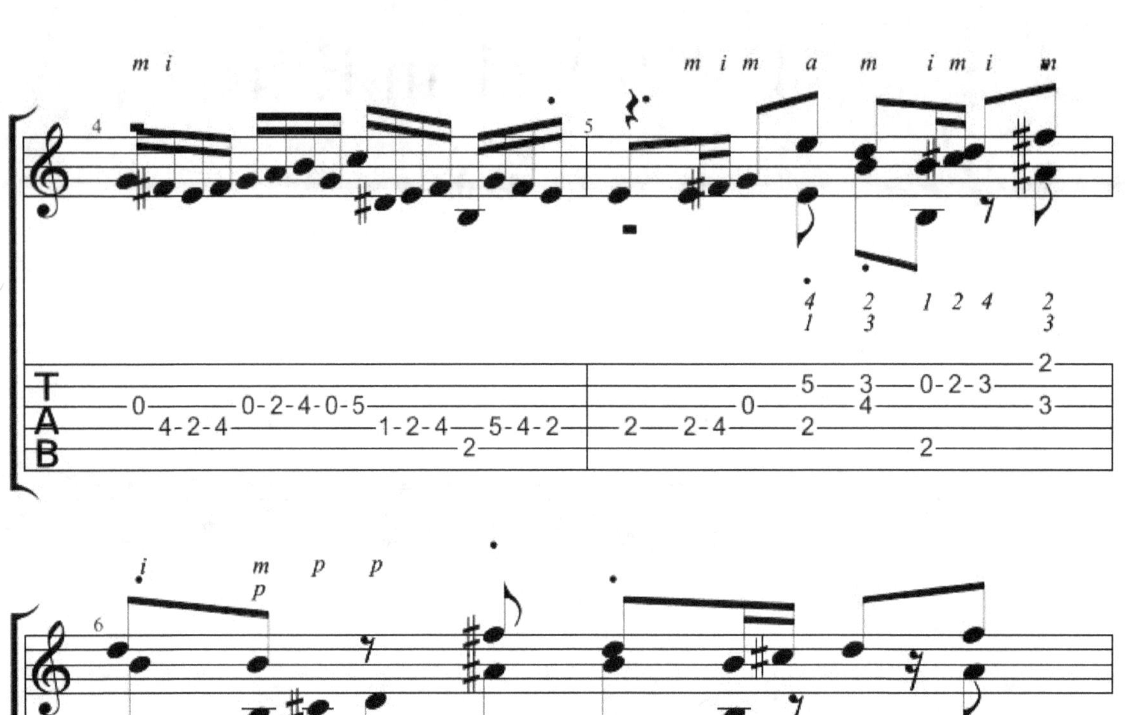
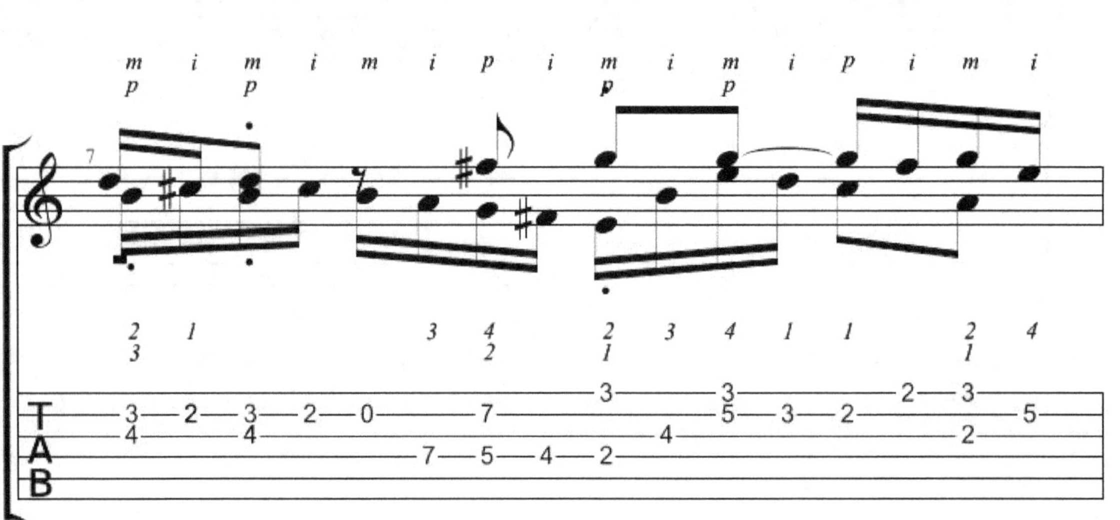

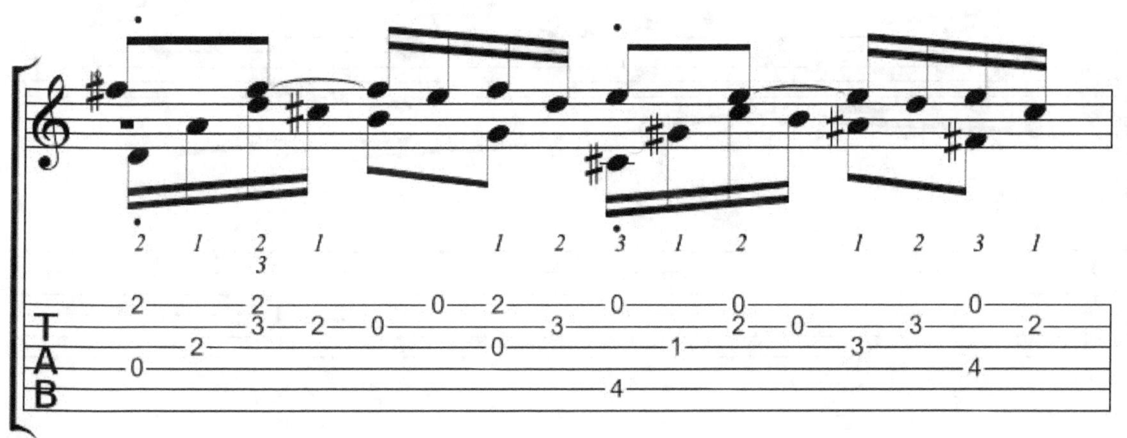

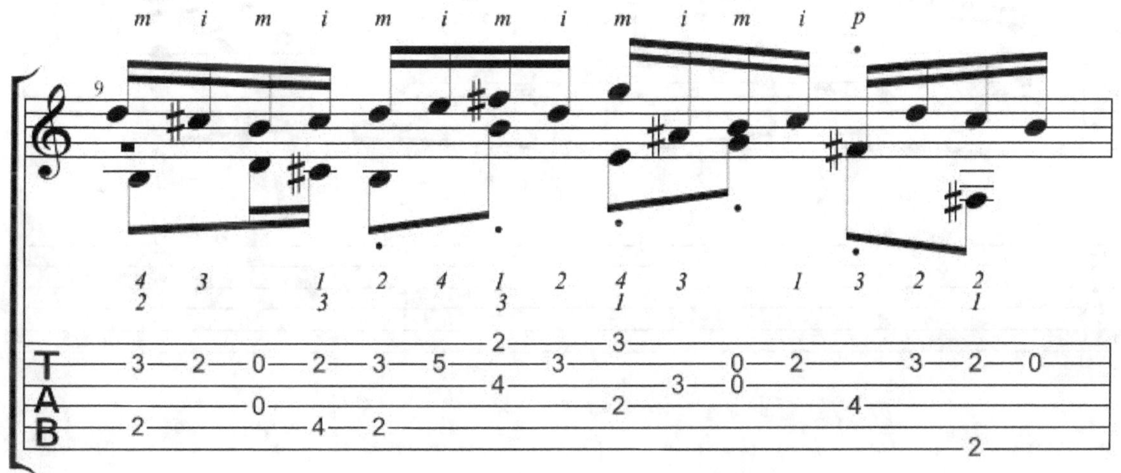
m i m i m i m i m i m i p

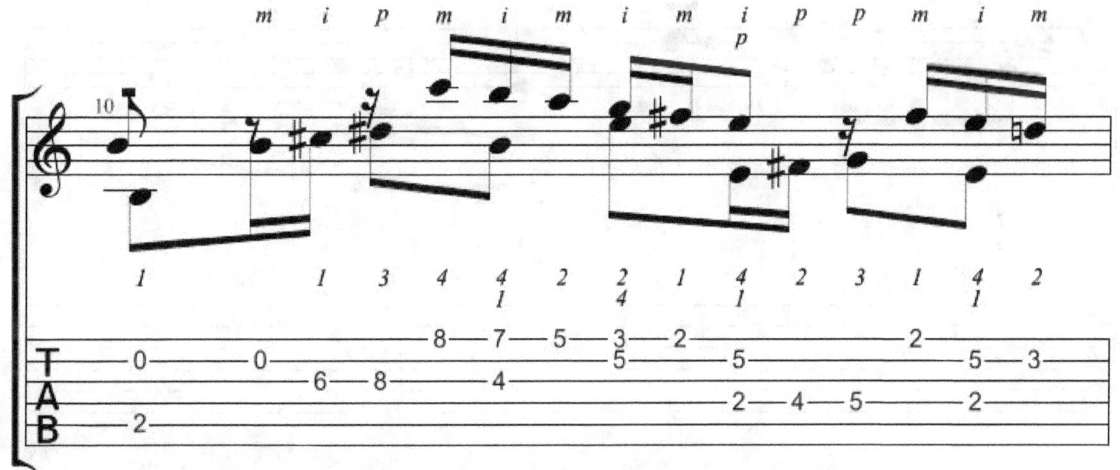
m i p m i m i m i p p p m i m

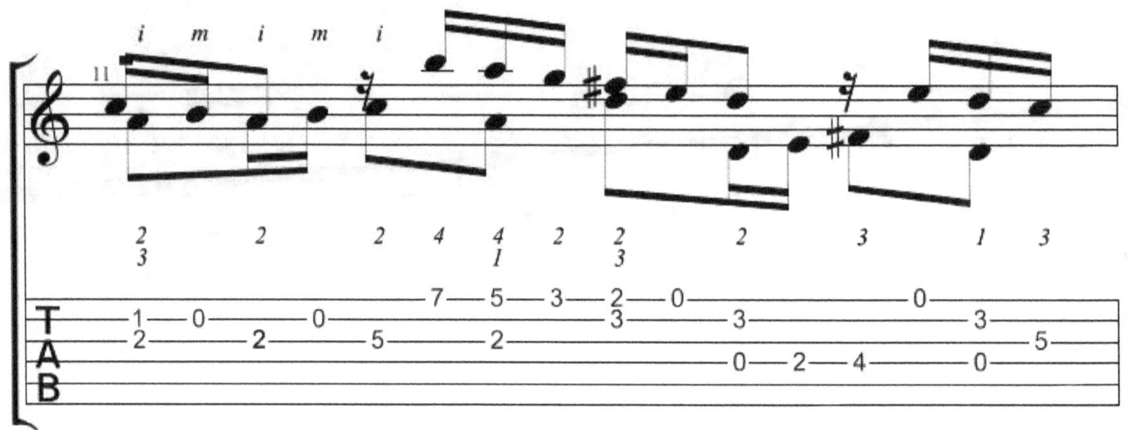

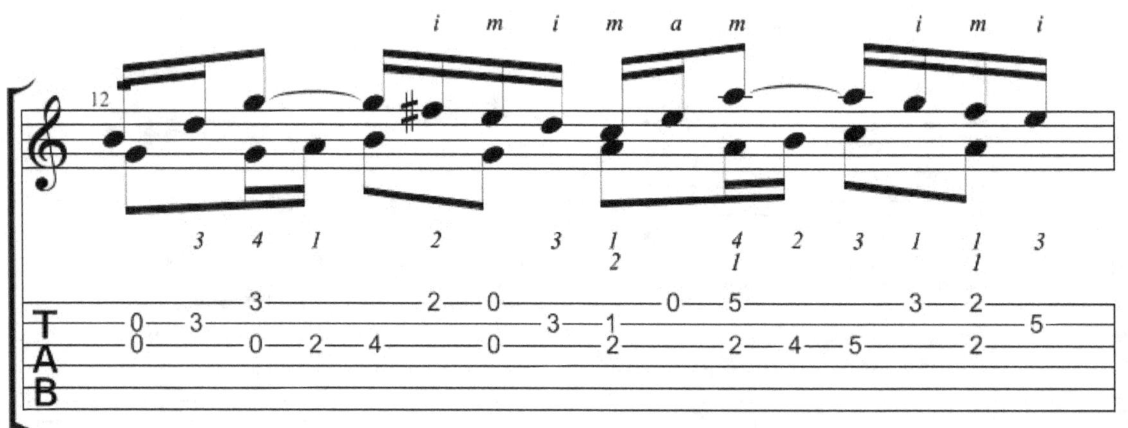

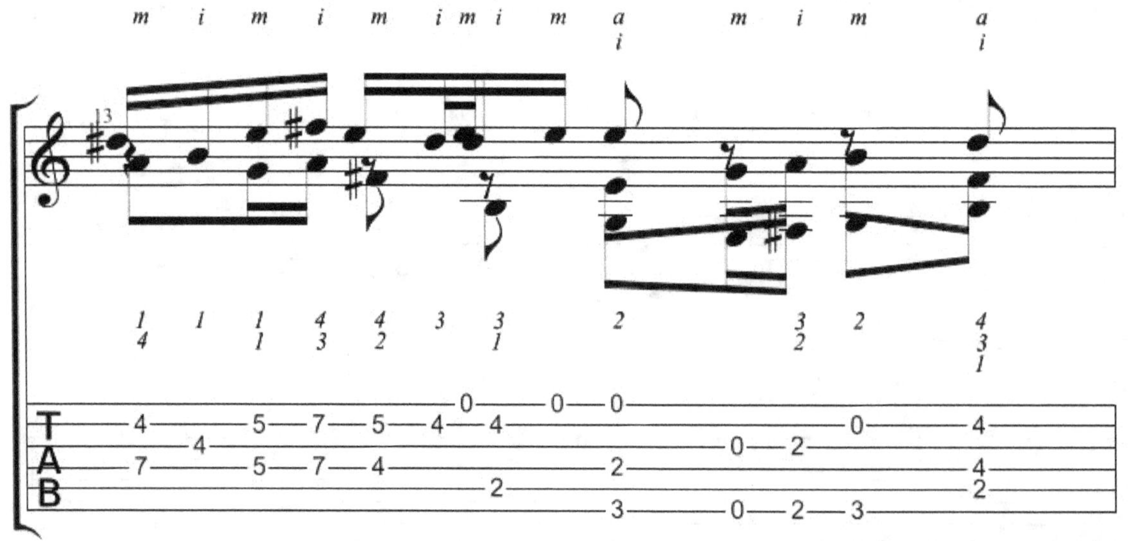

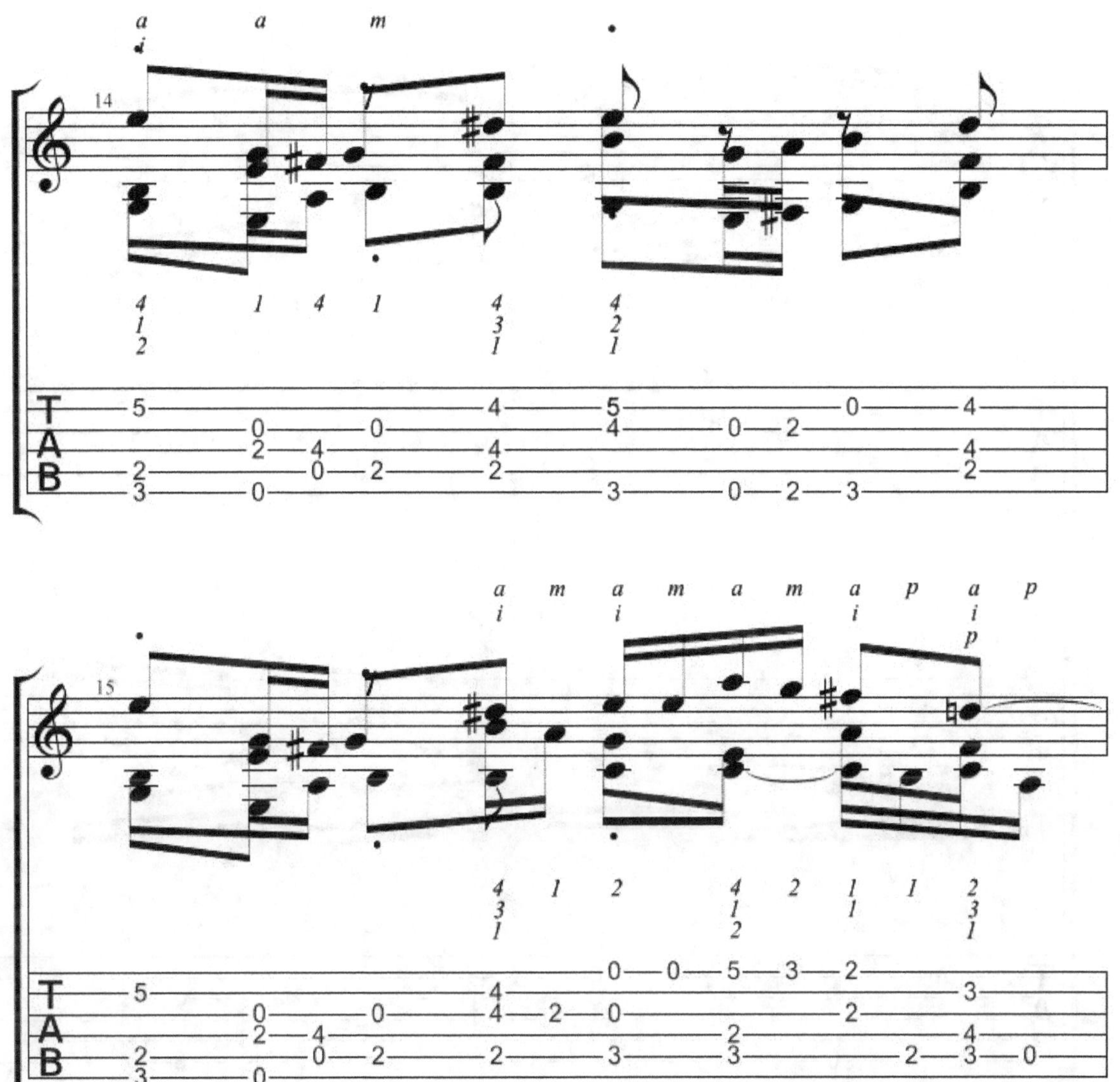

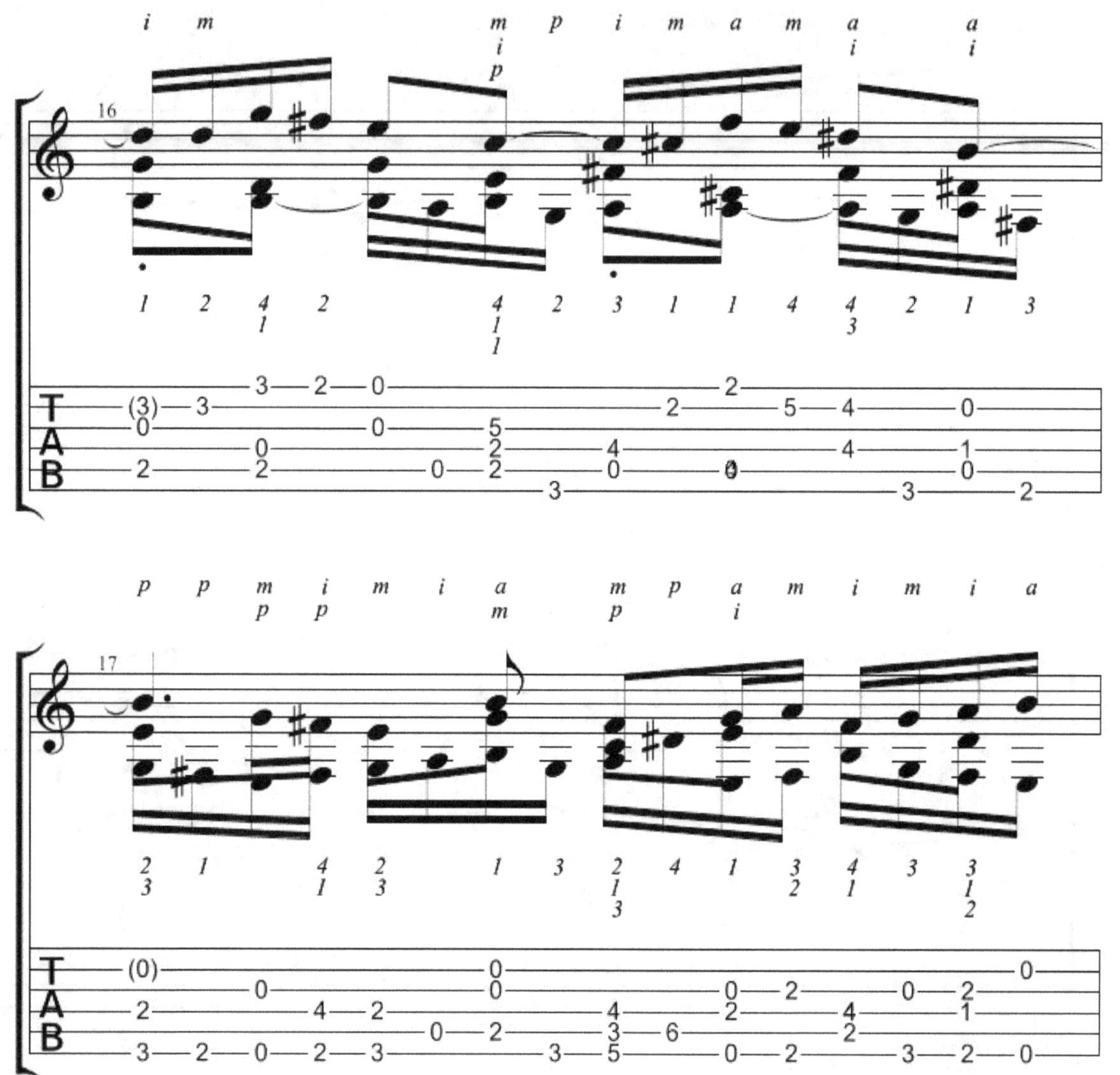

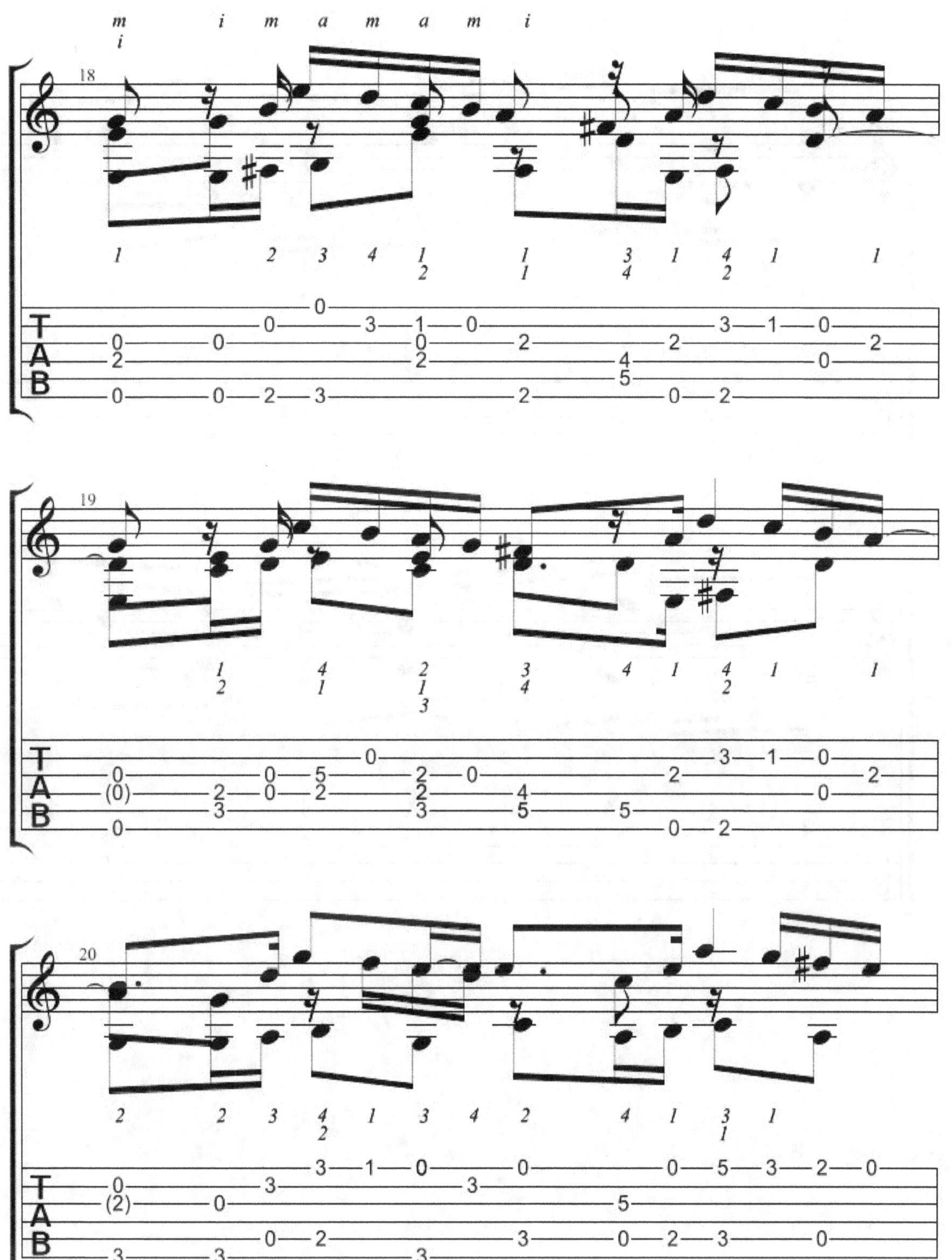

m i m a m a m i
i
18
19
20
7/20

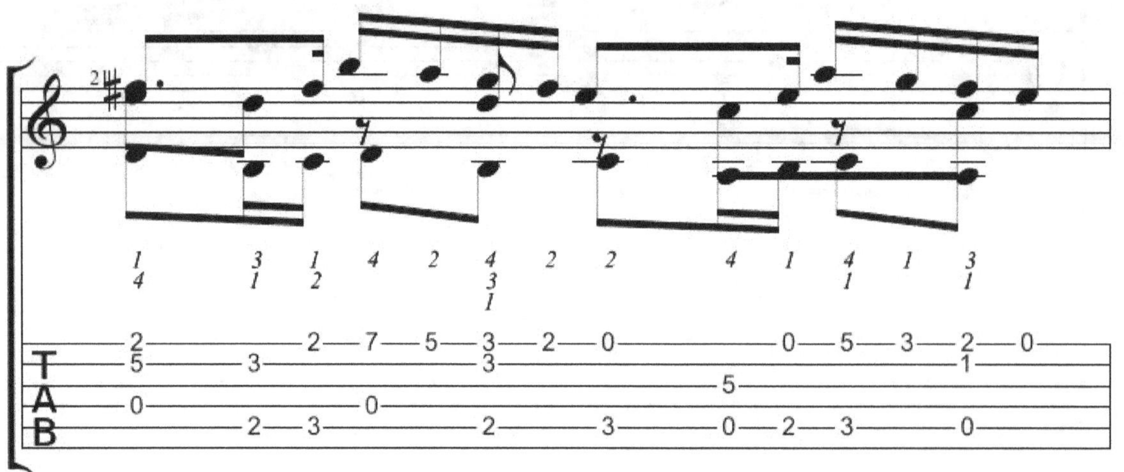

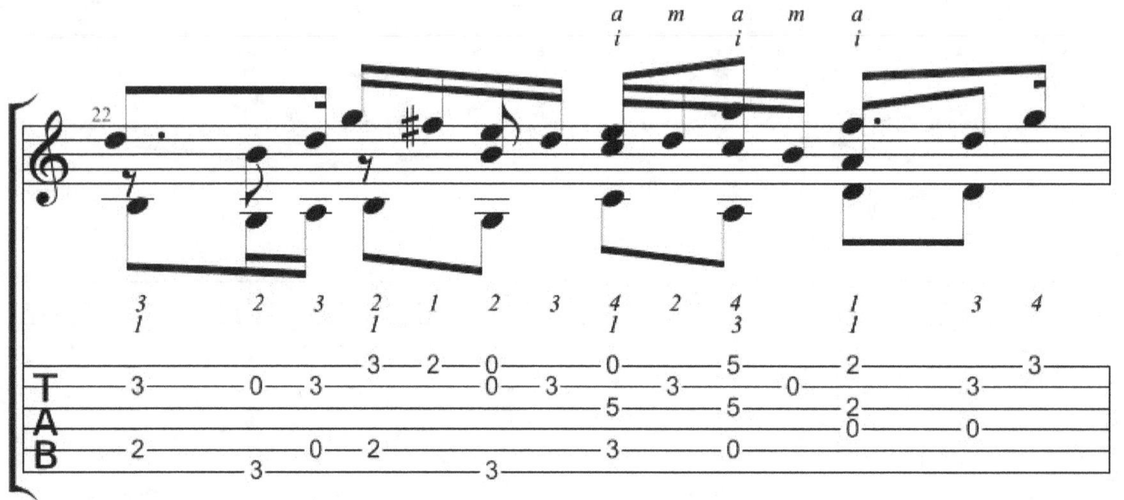

a m a m a
i i i

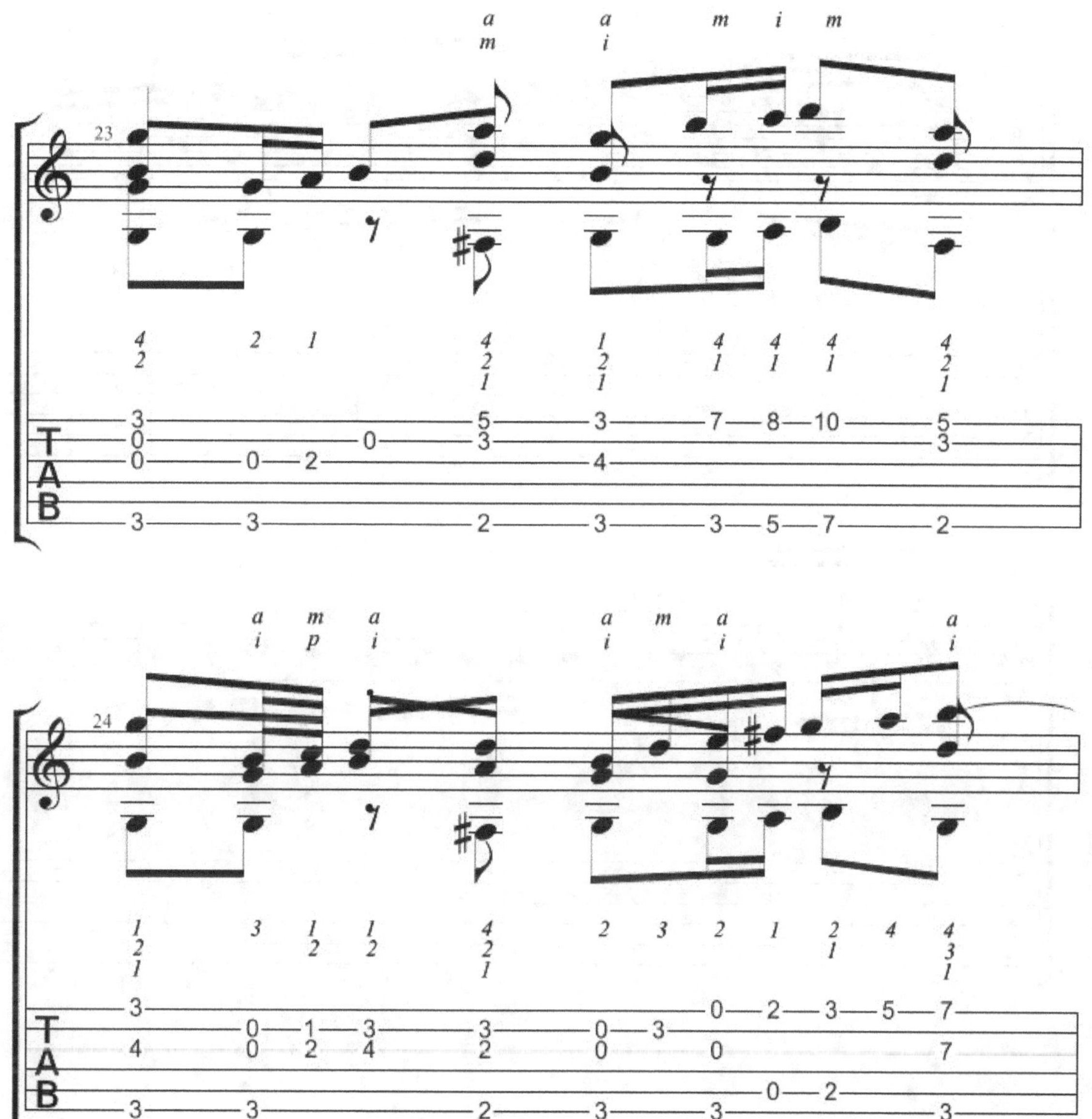

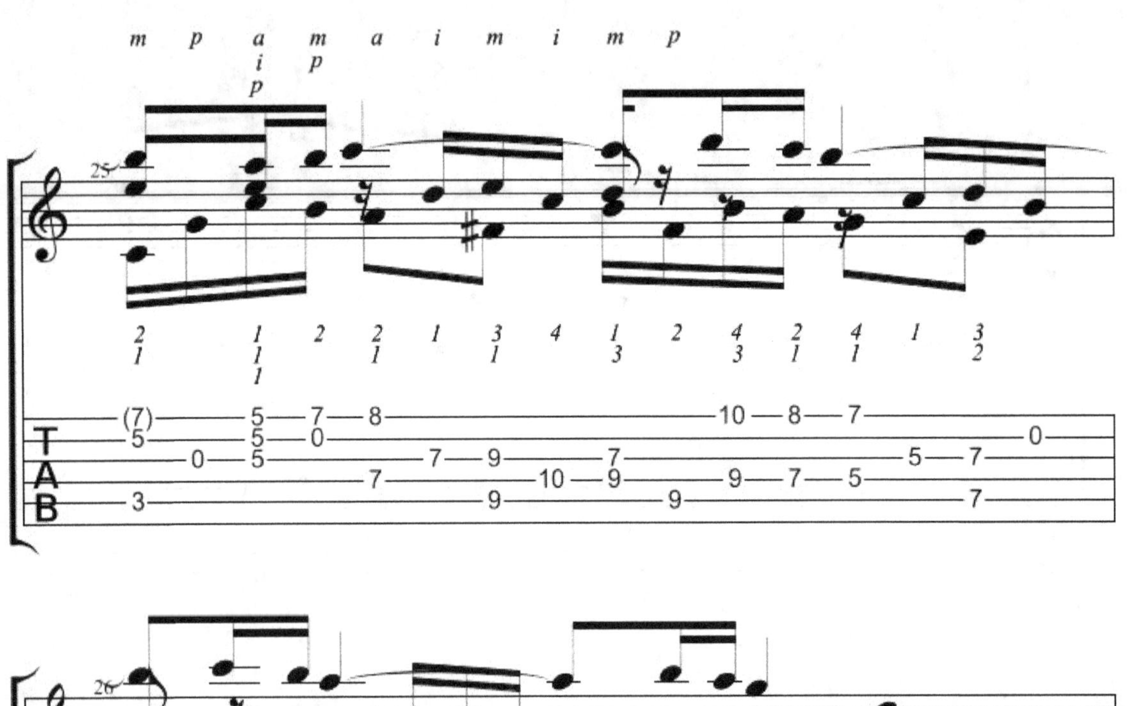
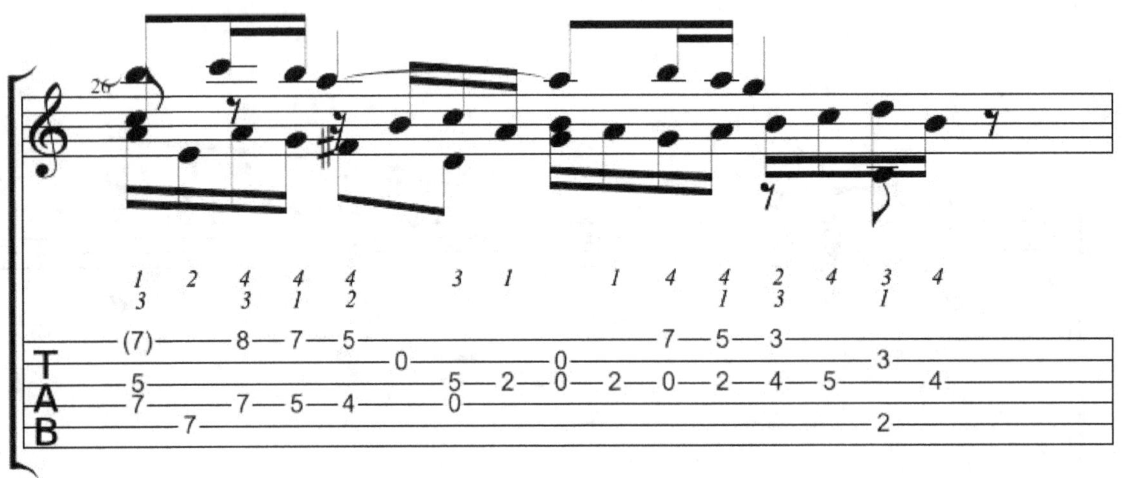

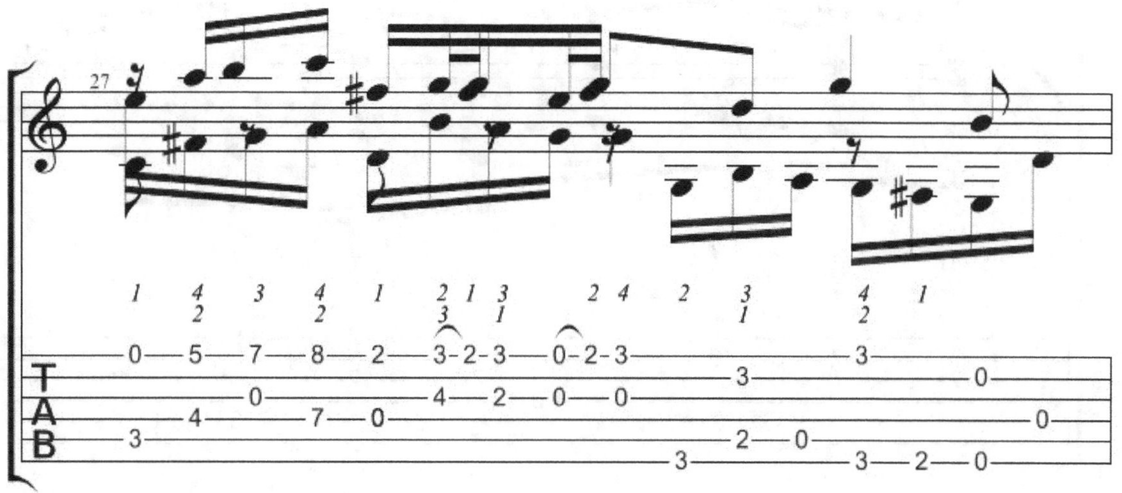
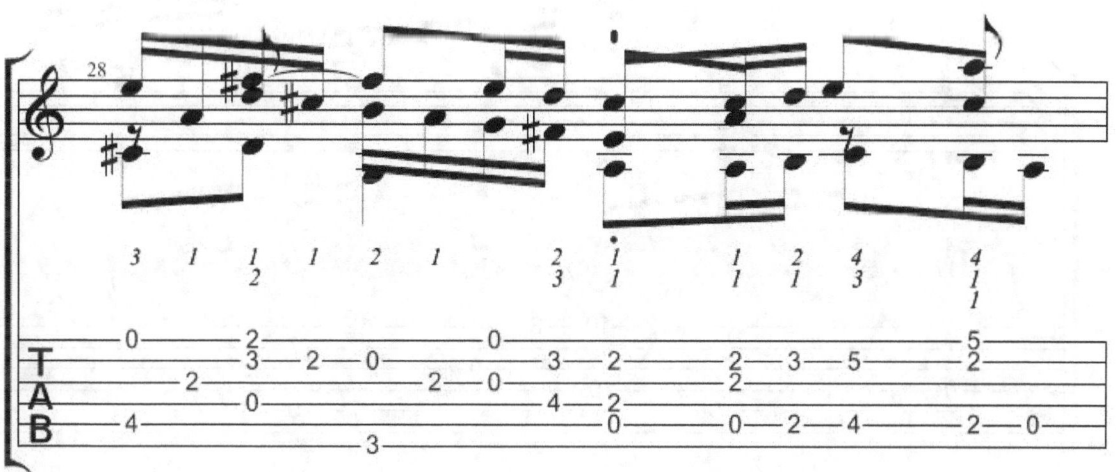

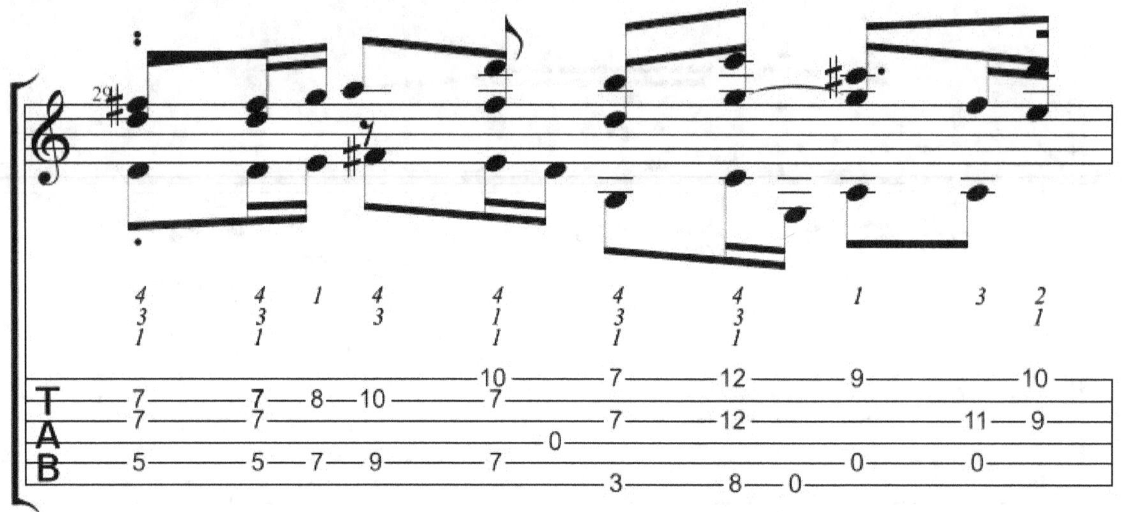

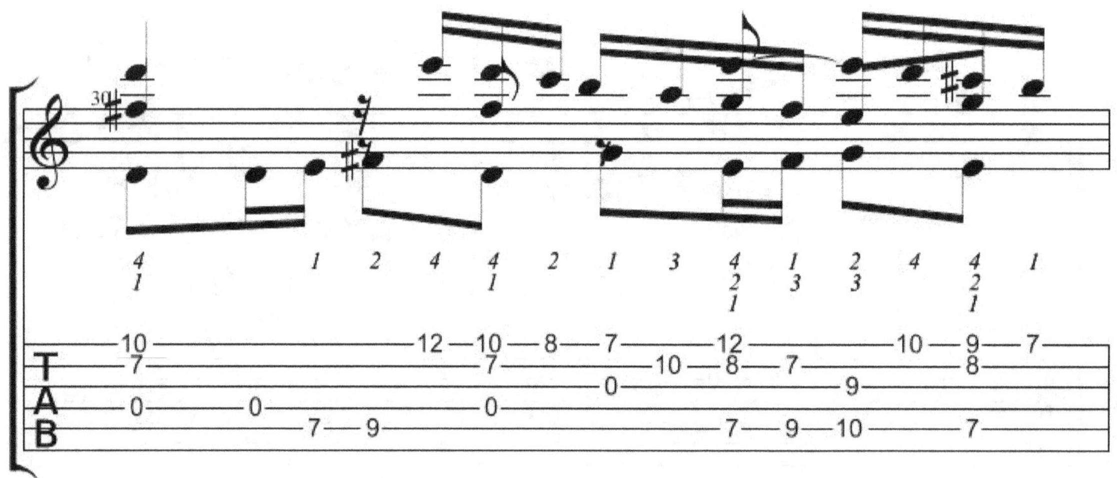

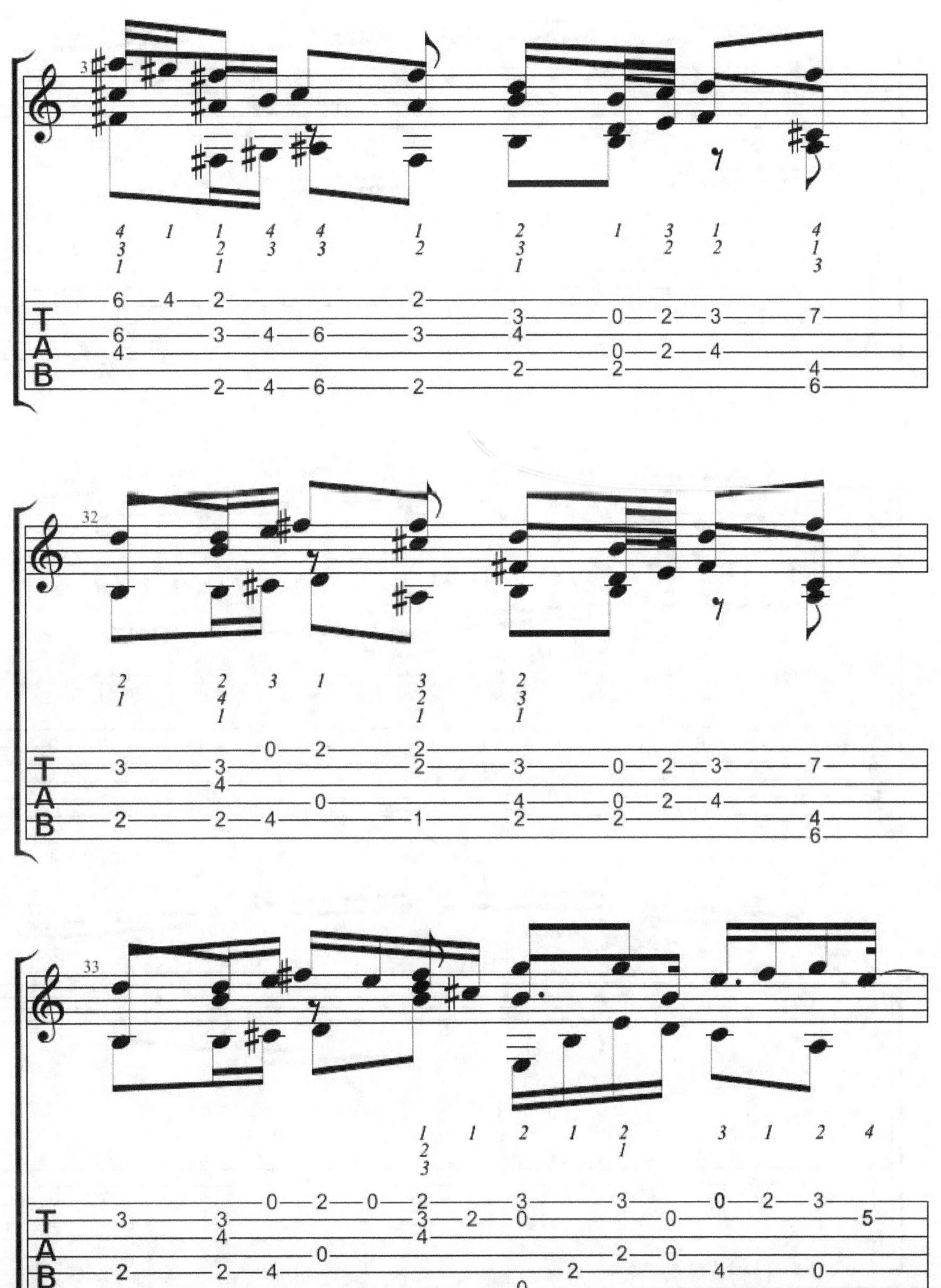

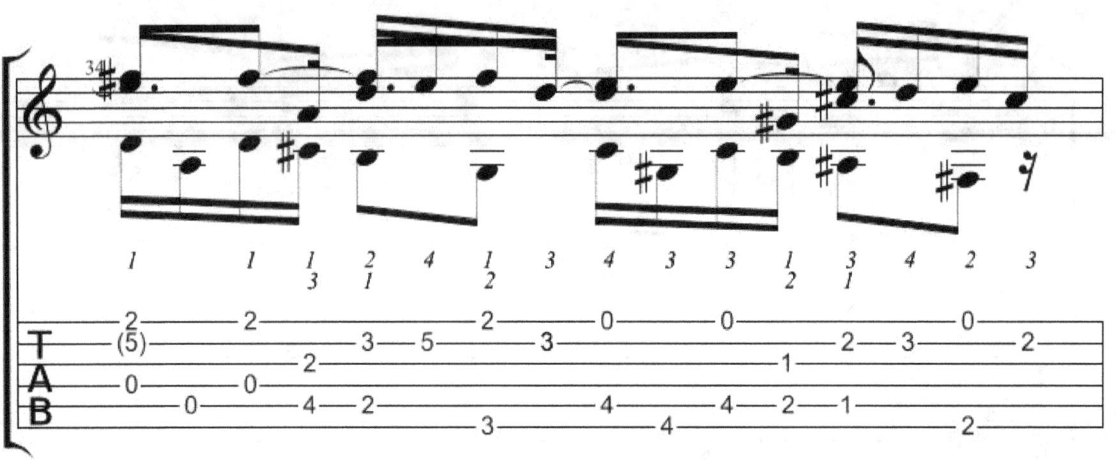

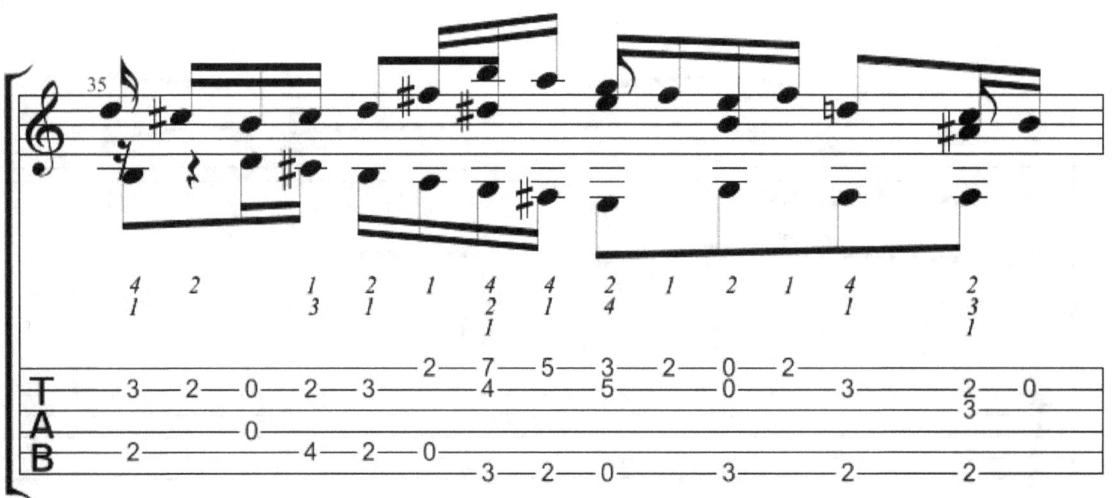

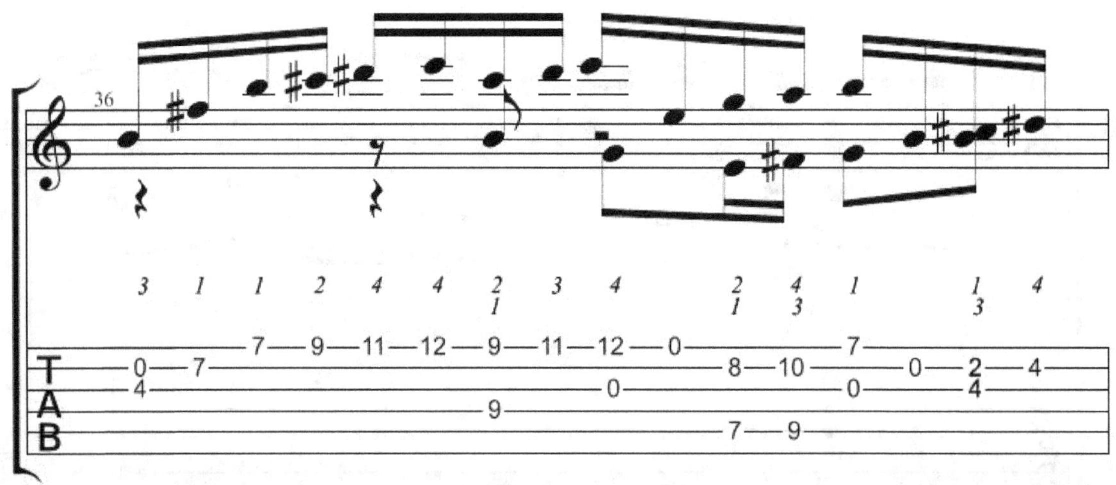

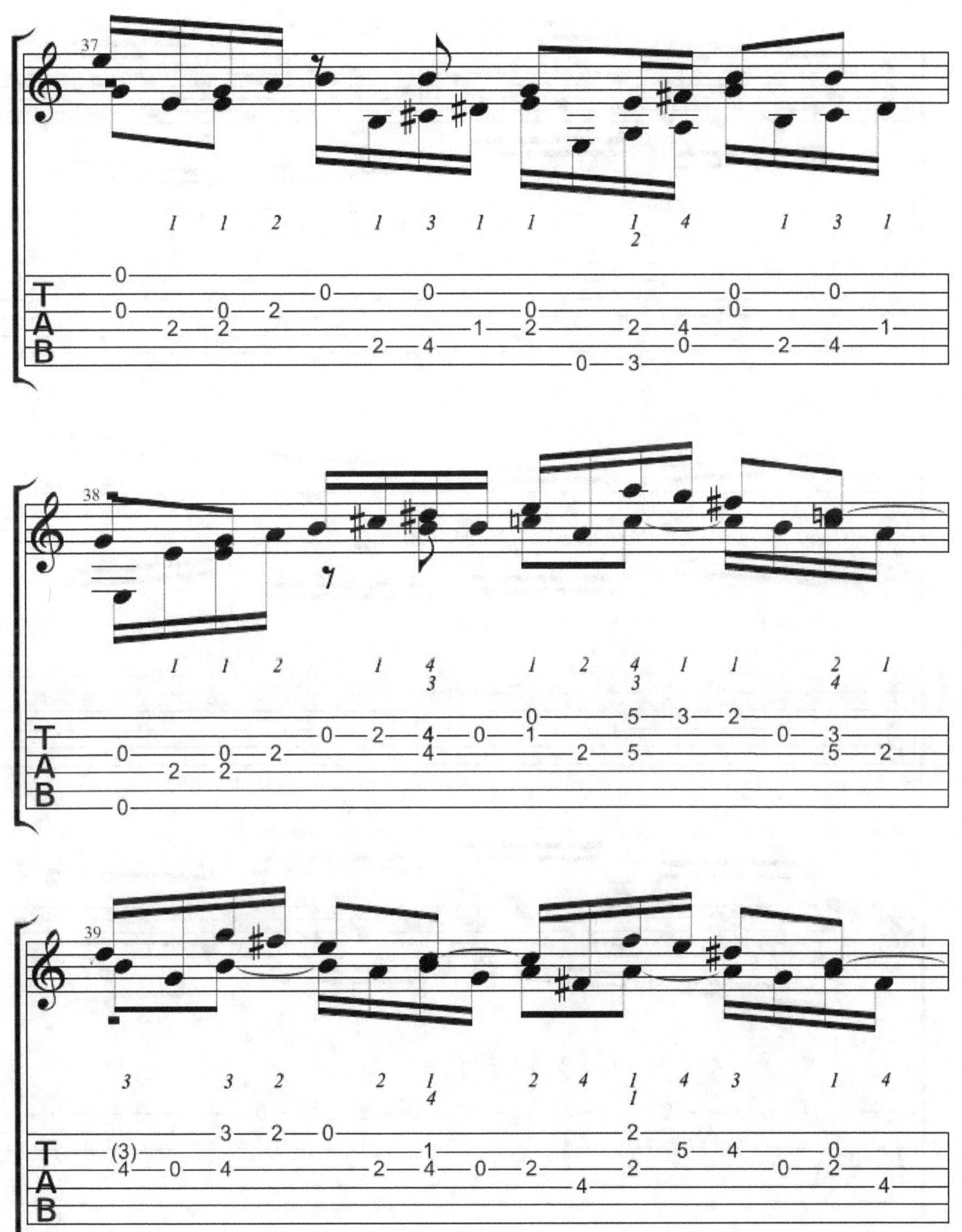

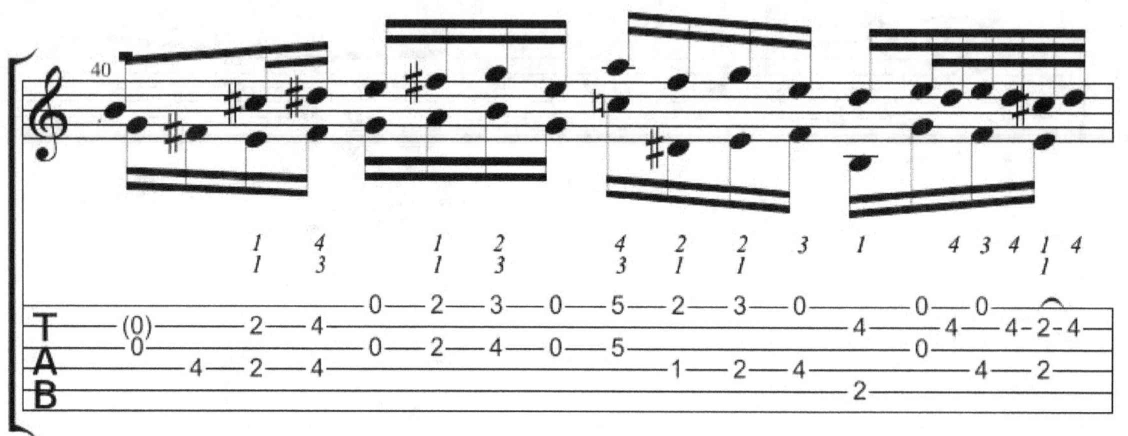

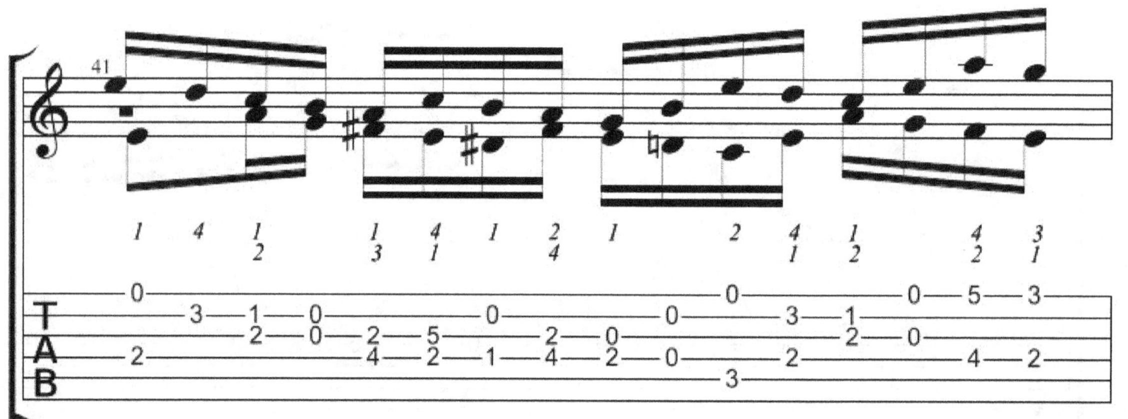

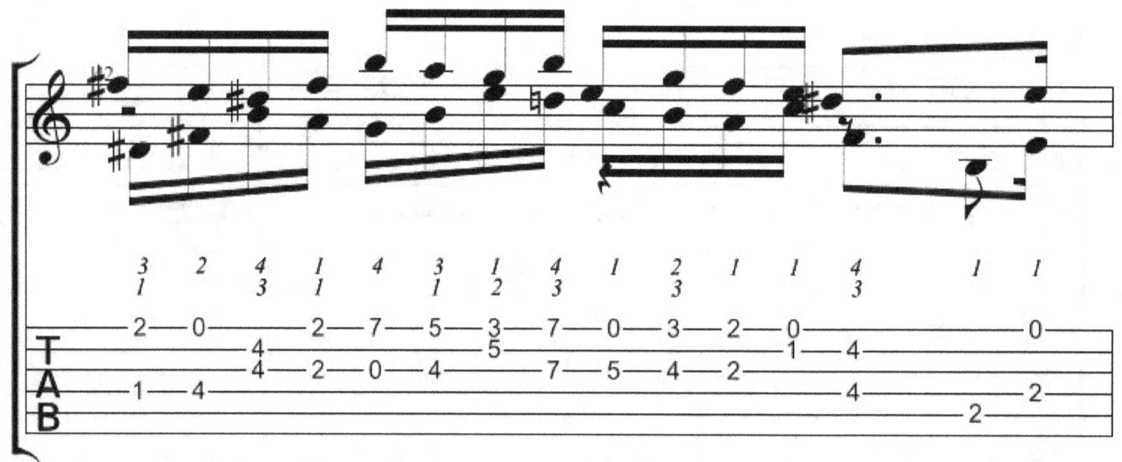

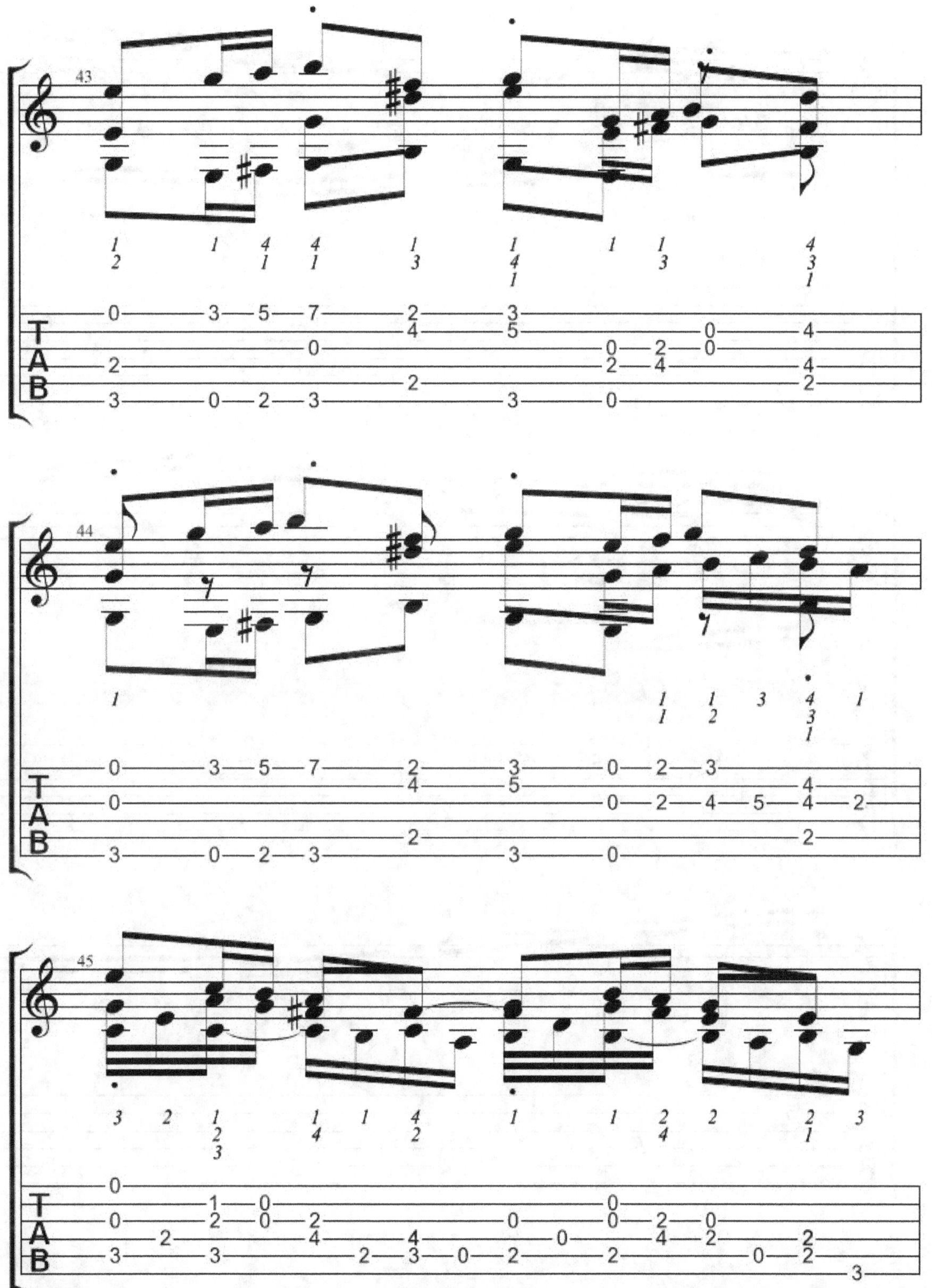

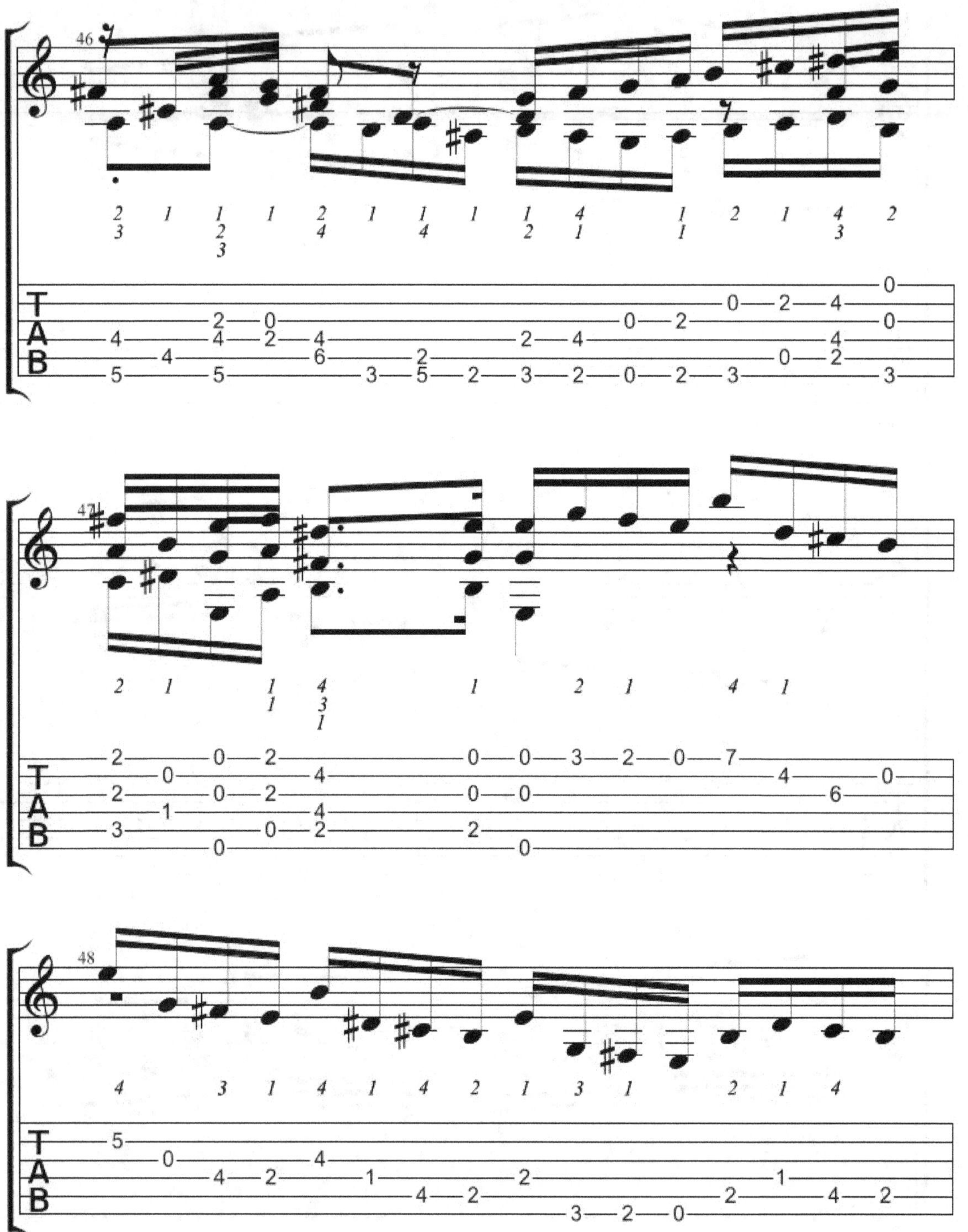

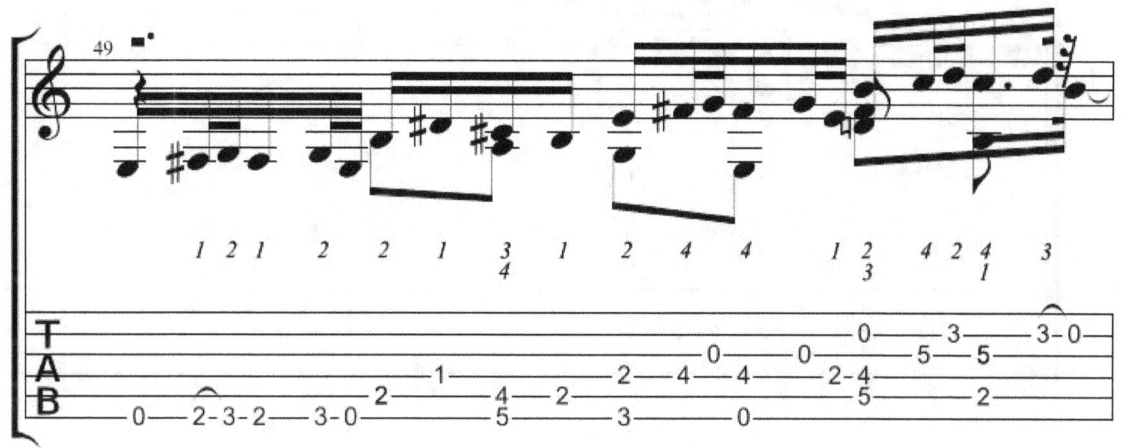

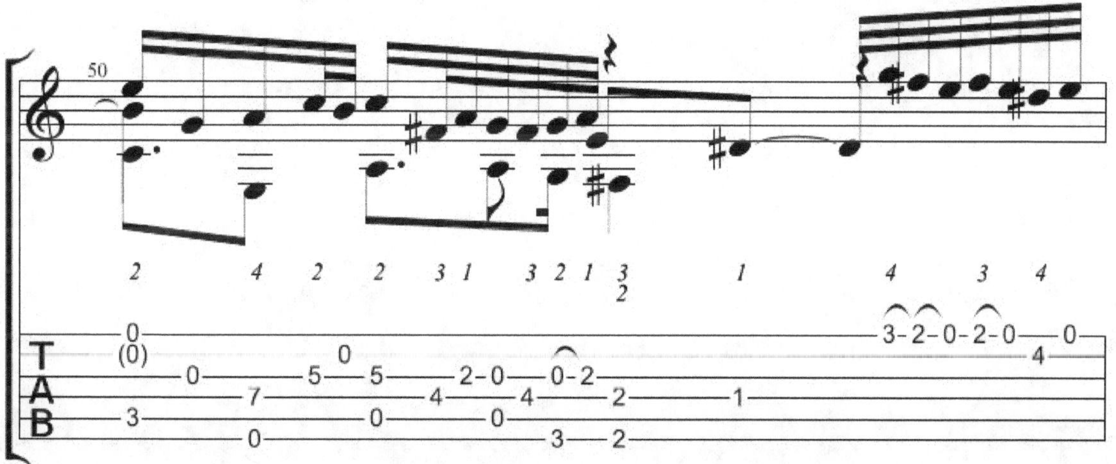

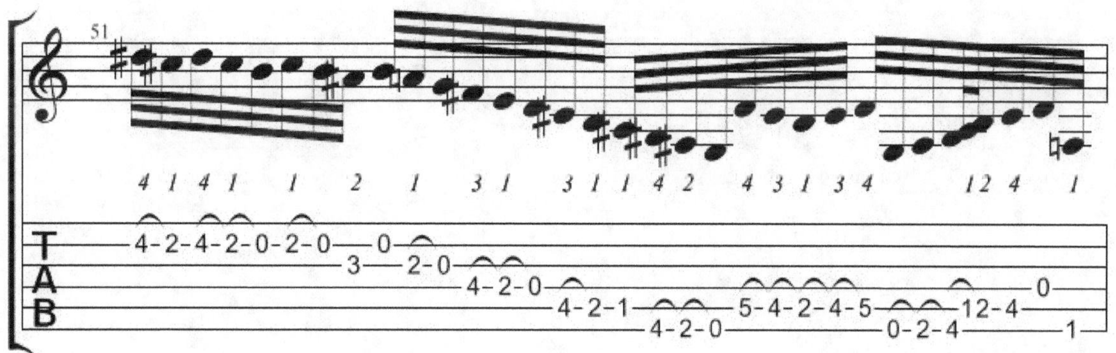

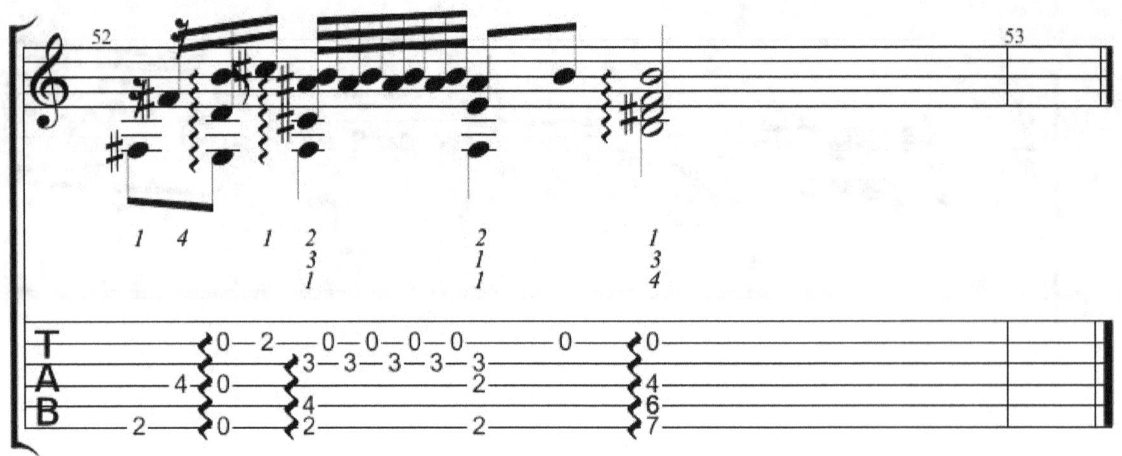